a poem freshens the world

—*ted kooser*

How to Read a Poem

based on the Billy Collins poem
"introduction to poetry"

tania runyan

FG *field guide series*

ts T. S. Poetry Press • New York

T. S. Poetry Press
Ossining, New York
Tspoetry.com

This book includes various references from or to the following
brands & sources: *The Poetry Home Repair Manual: Practical
Advice for Beginning Poets*, Ted Kooser, University of Nebraska
Press (2005); *BuzzFeed*, BuzzFeed, Inc; iPad, Apple; Power-
Point, Microsoft; "Texas Flood," "I'm Crying," and "Lenny,"
by Stevie Ray Vaughan, from the album *Texas Flood*, Epic
Records (1983); Vaseline, Unilever; Big Bird, Sesame Street,
Sesame Workshop.

Cover image by Claire Burge claireburge.com

ISBN 978-0-9898542-2-1

Library of Congress Cataloging-in-Publication Data:
Runyan, Tania
        [Nonfiction/Poetry.]
        How to Read a Poem: Based on the Billy Collins Poem
            "Introduction to Poetry"
        ISBN 978-0-9898542-2-1
        Library of Congress Control Number: 2013957013

*for laura, who works harder at loving poetry
than anyone I know*

Contents

Introduction

How to read a poem. A lot of books want to teach you just that. How is this one different?

Think of it less as an instructional book and more as an invitation. For the reader new to poetry, this guide will open your senses to the combined craft and magic known as *poems*. For the well versed, if you will, this book might make you fall in love again.

For many of us, poetry is difficult and unapproachable. Or perhaps we manage well enough, but it feels like so much work—another academic exercise to check off our lists. If poetry requires that much effort, it certainly doesn't feel like something to enjoy, something to curl up with by the fire (or pool).

Whatever your story, I'm going to try to trick you into becoming a better reader of poetry by having fun.

In this book, you will not answer comprehension questions or discuss literary terms directly. Rather, the focus will be to engage you with the poem. Sure, you will become intimately entwined with alliteration, enjambment, and metaphor, but for now, defining and memorizing terms is not important. We're not going on a scavenger hunt for literary devices. We're first and foremost taking a journey to deepen your relationship with poems. This is not about finding answers, decoding lines, or being smart. It's about paying attention to poems. And poems paying attention to you.

You're invited on a journey. Will you RSVP *yes*?

The Reading Soul

Poetry, I have a confession to make. I'm a poet, with two degrees and many editorial positions to my credit, but I don't always want to spend time with you. Unlike Facebook and Twitter, who wave their hands wildly for my attention, you sit in the corner of the garden like that quiet, intricate columbine by the bench.

Come and read me. Not as an editor working through a stack of review copies, but as you, a reading soul. There is so much to talk about. Please, just shut up and take a seat.

I grab my coffee and flip open my iPad®. Just one more *BuzzFeed* article, Poetry. Then I'll read you.

I know I've complained that you're too much work, but it's a dumb excuse. Life *without* you is too much work—trying to make meaning among all the empty words distracting me from, as Mary Oliver calls it, my "one wild and precious life."

So teach me how to spend time with you again. Let's rekindle the passion I had before I became a poetry professional, before I knew any better.

Maybe Billy Collins can help.

Introduction to Poetry

I ask them to take a poem
and hold it up to the light
like a color slide

or press an ear against its hive.

I say drop a mouse into a poem
and watch him probe his way out,

or walk inside the poem's room
and feel the walls for a light switch.

I want them to waterski
across the surface of a poem
waving at the author's name on the shore.

But all they want to do
is tie the poem to a chair with rope
and torture a confession out of it.

They begin beating it with a hose
to find out what it really means.

— Billy Collins, from *The Apple That Astonished Paris*

Without beating Collins's well-known poem to death (wouldn't *that* be ironic?), I'm going to use it as a field guide for my own reading. Join me as I walk through several poems' rooms, flip some light switches to see better how to live my wild life, and tell about it.

1

Hold It to the Light: Imagery

Billy Collins's "Introduction to Poetry" challenges us not to analyze a poem, but to enter it, live with it, and make it a part of us.

In this chapter, I'm going to explore how Collins's first stanza can help us fall in love with poetry's dazzler: imagery.

> I ask them to take a poem
> and hold it up to the light
> like a color slide

Collins tells us to hold the poem up to the light. A younger reader may ask how exactly one can hold a large piece of playground equipment up to the sun, but the slide in this stanza is supposed to make us think of images. In the ancient days before digital cameras and PowerPoint®, people turned their photo negatives into slides to create slide shows. My best sources (um, *Wikipedia* writers) describe a slide as "a specially mounted individual transparency intended for projection onto a screen using a slide projector." Color slides are small, just 2×2 inches, and when people want to see the image without a projector, they must hold it to a light source, squint a bit, turn it to get a good look.

So how do you hold a poem up to the light? Just look at it from several angles, and don't worry about what the poem means.

Consider the images in the following poem:

The Moon Is a Comma,
a Pause in the Sky

We stand creekside. It's tomorrow
somewhere else and we're discussing
if we'll have a tomorrow together.
Coyotes howl in the woods behind us.
We keep waiting for one
of us to save the other, but we're quiet.
We can leave here still
a family or we can walk separate
directions. We listen to the chorus,
coyotes and baby coyotes, a tornado
of cries as if they're circling.

— Kelli Russell Agodon, from *Letters from the
Emily Dickinson Room*

We can find a few pictures here: the moon as a comma,
the creek, the tornado of cries. The last image stands out as
the central element, the climax the poem drives toward. Let's
take a look:

....We listen to the chorus,
coyotes and baby coyotes, a tornado
of cries as if they're circling.

How do we open ourselves to this moment, this image?

Here are some guidelines:

1) What do I see, hear, smell, taste or touch on the first, basic level of reading?

Despite its name, imagery refers to all the senses. Upon reading these words, I hear a collection of coyotes' voices: the lower howls of the parents, the higher yelps of the babies. I see and feel the soft, silvery brown fur of the animals circling in a pack. They move intently but gently (they've got babies along), with slinking, deliberate legs. I also see the silvery brown funnel of a tornado touching down.

2) What does the image remind me of?

After taking the time to appreciate the image with my senses, I allow my mind to associate. Freely. What does this picture remind me of in my life and in the world? Here are just a few:

• A dedicated but bad choir
• My children as babies
• My new dog
• Packs of hunting canines in nature videos and the pink carcasses they chew on
• Lying in bed at night and hearing coyotes howl in the woods
• Destructive tornadoes that strike the Midwest

3) How do I feel?

Now I give myself permission to feel what I feel. Obviously, there is no right way to do this, so I begin by revisiting parts of the poem. The last images certainly seem ominous. Circling coyotes? A tornado?

As I spend some time with these canines, I feel strangely threatened and secure at once. Coyotes howling near my neighborhood mean certain death to smaller animals wandering the night. Yet, the howls remind me I am not alone—that there is more going on than my life and its (often small) problems. The animals move through the night together as a strong family pack. Their circling tornado of cries, then, is both a trap and an embrace—both danger and comfort.

How do these feelings affect my experience with the poem as a whole?

Of course, neither Collins nor I would recommend reading an image out of context without returning to its larger poetic home, so how do those sensory experiences, associations, and emotions help us understand the poem? Let me respond not with answers, but with more questions:

• How apt is this family to have "a tomorrow together"? Are they a strong enough pack themselves?
• Can one of them save the other? Will they remain quiet as their destruction looms or make the move toward safety?
• Will they stay together as a family or split apart? What is more likely as the eye of the tornado closes in?
• Ultimately, will this troubled night in their lives, this comma of moon in the sky awaiting the next clause, make or break them?
• How have I experienced the same thrilling desperation of conflict?

Now that I've spent some time with the coyotes, I know how I would answer these questions. What about you?

Stepping Out

Are you ready to explore? As you read, scribble on, and discuss the following poems, allow these tips to guide you:

• What do you see, hear, smell, taste, or touch when you read the poem through the first time?

• Choose a few key images. For each image, ask yourself the following:

—What does the image remind me of?
—How do I feel?
—How does this feeling fit in with my experience of the poem as a whole?

Prelude

In the pause between spring rain
a woman pirouettes in a field.

Her skin is a thousand mirrors.

Sholeh Wolpé

Loss

She carries a miniature portrait
in the pocket of her jacket,
south/southwest
of her heart,
where it bumps
above the ribcage,
a little window
the size of a salmon fillet
and framed in black walnut.

It's just the sort of thing
Sir Walter Raleigh may have carried
as an icon of his Queen.

It is painted in straw-yellow,
a field of grass with circles
of black ash settled,
like snow between dry blades.

We see only the field:
the subject of the portrait is elsewhere.

Benjamin Myers

The Eagle

He clasps the crag with crooked hands;
Close to the sun in lonely lands,
Ringed with the azure world, he stands.

The wrinkled sea beneath him crawls;
He watches from his mountain walls,
And like a thunderbolt he falls.

Lord Alfred Tennyson

The Body Reinvented

How odd to wake up at fifty
in this body of loose boards
and tumbling bricks

with its hair like chipped paint
and its bleary breasts
like the eyes of exhausted yaks,
its back like a suitcase
full of iron nightgowns,
and its boarded-up womb—
a museum awash with ghosts.

But a body still wearing
that sly mauve dress
and dancing shoes frantic as castanets

that refuse to scrape off
or be hauled away
or dissolved in the fumes of time's turpentine
    oh, won't you come dance with this body
with its songs that keep sprouting
like a million brash buds
and its face of unquenchable
five-year-old's joy
hardening into a diamond.

Pamela Miller

Blizzard

Snow:
years of anger following
hours that float idly down —
the blizzard
drifts its weight
deeper and deeper for three days
or sixty years, eh? Then
the sun! a clutter of
yellow and blue flakes —
Hairy looking trees stand out
in long alleys
over a wild solitude.
The man turns and there —
his solitary track stretched out
upon the world.

William Carlos Williams

In a London Drawingroom

The sky is cloudy, yellowed by the smoke.
For view there are the houses opposite
Cutting the sky with one long line of wall
Like solid fog: far as the eye can stretch
Monotony of surface & of form
Without a break to hang a guess upon.
No bird can make a shadow as it flies,
For all is shadow, as in ways o'erhung
By thickest canvass, where the golden rays
Are clothed in hemp. No figure lingering
Pauses to feed the hunger of the eye
Or rest a little on the lap of life.
All hurry on & look upon the ground,
Or glance unmarking at the passers by
The wheels are hurrying too, cabs, carriages
All closed, in multiplied identity.
The world seems one huge prison-house & court
Where men are punished at the slightest cost,
With lowest rate of colour, warmth & joy.

George Eliot

End of the Comedy

Eleven o'clock, and the curtain falls.
The cold wind tears the strands of illusion;
The delicate music is lost
In the blare of home-going crowds
And a midnight paper.

The night has grown martial;
It meets us with blows and disaster.
Even the stars have turned shrapnel,
Fixed in silent explosions.
And here at our door
The moonlight is laid
Like a drawn sword.

Louis Untermeyer

Storm Ending

Thunder blossoms gorgeously above our heads,
Great, hollow, bell-like flowers,
Rumbling in the wind,
Stretching clappers to strike our ears . . .
Full-lipped flowers
Bitten by the sun
Bleeding rain
Dripping rain like golden honey—
And the sweet earth flying from the thunder.

Jean Toomer

Crossing 16

You came to my door in the dawn and sang; it angered me to
      be awakened from sleep, and you went away unheeded.
You came in the noon and asked for water; it vexed me in my
      work, and you were sent away with reproaches.
You came in the evening with your flaming torches.
You seemed to me like a terror and I shut my door.
Now in the midnight I sit alone in my lampless room and call
      you back whom I turned away in insult.

Rabindranath Tagore

Vernal Equinox

The scent of hyacinths, like a pale mist, lies between
    me and my book;
And the South Wind, washing through the room,
Makes the candle quiver.
My nerves sting at a spatter of rain on the shutter,
And I am uneasy with the thrusting of green shoots
Outside, in the night.
Why are you not here to overpower me with your tense and
    urgent love?

Amy Lowell

2

An Ear Against a Hive: Sound

In the last chapter, we explored how to fall in love with poetry's darling, imagery. Continuing to use Billy Collins's poem "Introduction to Poetry" as a stanza-by-stanza field guide for reading poetry, we'll now take a look at my personal favorite: sound.

Here is the entire second stanza. Ready?

> or press an ear against its hive

I've never pressed my ear to a literal beehive, but I've been close enough to a swarm of bees to feel that unsettling—yet delicious—hum in my bones. Sounds sock us in the gut, but we can't always explain why. Try explaining how and why we react so emotionally to a coyote's howl or a piece of music. We have our "pet" sounds, too, that delight us. A burbling coffee pot, a kid coloring with markers, people turning magazine pages in a waiting room—those sounds hold my attention.

"A Love Poem," by Benjamin Myers, is a celebration of sound itself.

A Love Poem

There is magic
in the way a woman hums,

sounds as soft as wet summer
nights. Soft as skin.

Remember —
the village women humming
before the storm,
those first shy drops of rain
hiding in their hair,
humming the way
earth will hum like a kettledrum
after the rain.

My grandmother hummed mountains
by revival tents
fluttering like the dove in the breeze
beside the singing river.

Now the woman who calls me hers
hums softly with the wind on the porch swing,
scent of honeysuckle settled behind her eyes.

The same song
swinging softly through the years.
She hums with my head
rested like morning in her lap,
and I know that song.

— Benjamin Myers, from *Elegy for Trains*

In the last chapter, I offered a few steps for how to get the most out of a poem's images (without "beating the poem with a hose," as Collins would say). This time, as we focus on sound, I'm going to ask you to do just one thing: read the poem. Aloud, with no music or TV in the background. At least three times. People don't read poetry aloud as much as they used to, but we must remember that for thousands of years, poems existed as an oral tradition. Poetry had to buzz to be remembered, to be worth repeating.

Allow me to take you through my journey of sound with "A Love Poem." Let's see what makes this sweet hive buzz.

First read

Upon my first reading, it's the *s*'s that get to me. The first stanza, alone, awakens my senses, especially these two lines:

> sounds as soft as wet summer
> nights. Soft as skin.

I love warm, rainy summer nights, when I can fall asleep to the sounds of rain slapping the gutters and splashing the maple leaves. The next morning, the water seems to steam and sizzle on the pavement as it heats up. Those wet summer nights are quite *s*-ish, aren't they? Then "soft as skin"—sensual as that summer rain. The sound is magical, isn't it? You can feel the softness and relief of the much-needed summer rain and the skin of the person you love. Then I arrive at these delicious lines:

> scent of honeysuckle settled behind her eyes.

> The same song
> swinging softly through the years.

The *s* sounds return like that magical rain, a song that crosses senses into the scent of honeysuckle and the movement of a swing.

Second read

My second time through the poem, I'm struck by its literal hum. The poem celebrates the power of a woman's hum, and many of the sounds themselves reflect that. The *n* and *m* sounds in "woman hums" vibrate in the mouth like a tremor, as do the sounds in "women humming/before the storm," "earth will hum like a kettledrum," and "My grandmother hummed mountains." Read those lines over and over. Don't they just reverberate in your throat? Is it any wonder that the hums of important women in the speaker's life have haunted him, beautifully, all these years?

Third read

My third time reading the poem aloud, I'm again taken in by the same lush, repeated sounds. (You can never read a beautiful poem too many times. It's like clicking the *repeat* button on your favorite song.) The softness, the hum, fills me with the comfort and promise of rain and the love of a familiar voice. What I notice this third time through, which I haven't noticed before, is the last line: "and I know that song."

Pretty simple, right? But I read that line over and over. What makes it feel so different from the other lines? First of all, each word is just one syllable, so the line does not possess the same fluid "hum" as most of the other lines. Secondly, this is one of the only lines that doesn't use some sort of alliteration (words starting with the same letter) or consonance (similar consonant sounds within words). There may be a bit of assonance (similar vowel sounds within words) in "know" and "song," but nothing as tightly knit as what we find in the other lines. In other words, this line stands out by *not* employing the softness and hum of the other lines—which is what makes it so perfect. The speaker knows this song so well, he is able to tell us directly, outside of the hum's trance, with confidence. The song of his loved ones is true, objective. It must be so.

Have I reached a "confession" or "answer" from this poem by reveling in its sounds? No, and I don't think I should. There is no formula for finding meaning in a poem by listening to it. Listening helps us attend. Listening heightens our experience by raising our awareness of our emotions. There is something about sounds that cannot be explained, and although I threw out literary terms like *alliteration*, *consonance*, and *assonance*, most poets write without consciously employing those techniques. Those "techniques" happen because they feel right, *because they are right*. As Benjamin Myers says elsewhere, "Maybe it's that sound doesn't happen in the mind at all but rather in the mouth." So this week, press your ear to the hive of a poem or two. Read and listen. Read and listen again. And see what your mouth and your ears tell you.

Stepping Out

Ready to listen up? The following poems offer a scrumptious feast of sounds. The guidelines are simple: Read once. Read twice. Read once more. Take your time, listen, and attend. Then hear how you feel.

The Night is Darkening Round Me

The night is darkening round me,
The wild winds coldly blow;
But a tyrant spell has bound me,
And I cannot, cannot go.

The giant trees are bending
Their bare boughs weighed with snow;
The storm is fast descending,
And yet I cannot go.

Clouds beyond clouds above me,
Wastes beyond wastes below;
But nothing drear can move me;
I will not, cannot go.

Emily Brontë

Tattoo

The light is like a spider.
It crawls over the water.
It crawls over the edges of the snow.
It crawls under your eyelids
And spreads its webs there—
Its two webs.

The webs of your eyes
Are fastened
To the flesh and bones of you
As to rafters or grass.

There are filaments of your eyes
On the surface of the water
And in the edges of the snow.

Wallace Stevens

Fabulous Ones

This poem is brought to you by the letter C.

Cattle egret, Big Bird says, *cetacean,*
the word squeaking like wet whale skin.

Big Bird keeps it real—his thug-life strut.

Do you like giants?
Only the small ones, the boy says.

Chinese catfish, cassava, cassowary.

He's an intellectual, spends his days off
in coffeehouses, crossing and uncrossing
the long orange tubes of his legs, discussing

Chomsky, conditional freedom, and *Cervantes*

with anyone who will listen. He marches
against the war, a thousand people
at his back, chanting

Catastrophe, cruise missile, children.

Big Bird refuses to fly south for the winter,
puts on his scarf and heads out the door.

You can't fool me, the boy says.
I know Big Bird's not real.
It's just a suit with a little bird inside.

Jeffrey Thomson

Jazz Fantasia

Drum on your drums, batter on your banjoes,
sob on the long cool winding saxophones.
Go to it, O jazzmen.

Sling your knuckles on the bottoms of the happy
tin pans, let your trombones ooze, and go husha-
husha-hush with the slippery sand-paper.

Moan like an autumn wind high in the lonesome treetops,
moan soft like you wanted somebody terrible, cry like a
racing car slipping away from a motorcycle cop, bang-bang!
you jazzmen, bang altogether drums, traps, banjoes, horns,
tin cans — make two people fight on the top of a stairway
and scratch each other's eyes in a clinch tumbling down
the stairs.

Can the rough stuff… now a Mississippi steamboat pushes
up the night river with a hoo-hoo-hoo-oo … and the green
lanterns calling to the high soft stars … a red moon rides
on the humps of the low river hills … go to it, O jazzmen.

Carl Sandburg

Matinee

After the biopsy,
after the bone scan,
after the consult and the crying,

for a few hours no one could find them,
not even my sister,
because it turns out

they'd gone to the movies.
Something tragic was playing,
something epic,

and so they went to the comedy
with their popcorn
and their cokes,

the old wife whispering everything twice,
the old husband
cupping a palm to his ear,

as the late sun lit up an orchard
behind the strip mall,
and they sat in the dark holding hands.

Patrick Phillips

The Lake Isle of Innisfree

I will arise and go now, and go to Innisfree,
And a small cabin build there, of clay and wattles made:
Nine bean-rows will I have there, a hive for the honey-bee;
And live alone in the bee-loud glade.

And I shall have some peace there, for peace comes
        dropping slow,
Dropping from the veils of the morning to where the
        cricket sings;
There midnight's all a glimmer, and noon a purple glow,
And evening full of the linnet's wings.

I will arise and go now, for always night and day
I hear lake water lapping with low sounds by the shore;
While I stand on the roadway, or on the pavements grey,
I hear it in the deep heart's core.

William Butler Yeats

Petit à Petit L'Oiseau Fait Son Nid

Little by little, they say,
the bird makes its nest.
I have been making mine
in silvered hemlocks, time
after time; today I used a red
thread I found near the garden.

I used to dream of living in a garden,
listening to words white orchids say
to emerald hummingbirds, red-
throated, stealing gold for nests
the size of women's thimbles, time
beating between breaths, a rhythm mine

could never find trapped, as in a mine
long hollowed, tapped black garden
that metamorphosed over time,
caught sounds of earth-on-earth say,
Come bed yourself on rock-hard nest,
turn death to sapphire, diamond, ruby red.

Rumor spreads: inside the earth is red,
molten, thrusting gold like mine
into the sun, into evening's nest
that sits above an empty garden
where orchids do not say
it is time

it is time
to ravel rays from ravished dreams, red
and unremembered; it is time to say
what is yours and what is mine
it is time to turn the garden
into earth, find fool's gold for a nest.

I have been making such a nest,
little by little, time after time,
I have been dreaming near a garden
in threads of memories, ruby red.
I have been claiming what is mine
and inviting you to say

you want the nest, the gold turning red,
the time we knew was mine,
the garden waiting, for what you have to say.

L.L. Barkat

People

The great gold apples of night
Hang from the street's long bough
　　Dripping their light
On the faces that drift below,
On the faces that drift and blow
Down the night-time, out of sight
　　In the wind's sad sough.

The ripeness of these apples of night
Distilling over me
　　Makes sickening the white
Ghost-flux of faces that hie
Them endlessly, endlessly by
Without meaning or reason why
　　They ever should be.

D. H. Lawrence

It is the Wings

It is the wings that take the damage,
not the hollow, honeycomb bones,
but the hooked feather-barbs,
their slender shafts twisted,
skewed, singed, snapped open,
veins and muscles, tiny nerve endings
flayed: it is the wings
that bear the glory.

Claire Bateman

The Pants of Existence

Burn this light my
my, o my—
not in Kansas any less than
this place of fur spangles
dangling on the ankles
of fate like
bells of hells,
transforming the middle ear
to the inner circle of
laughter, where I crease
the pants of existence
and press the life out. If
only the socks matched!

Marci Rae Johnson & Yvonne Robery

3

Drop a Mouse In: Line

Using Billy Collins's "Introduction to Poetry" as our lodestar, we've been seeking the fullest experience of poetry. First, we held a poem up to the light like a color slide, as a way to enter its imagery. Then we pressed our ears against a poem's hive to revel in its delicious sounds. Now we will

> ...drop a mouse into a poem
> and watch him probe his way out.

As if dealing with the last chapter's beehive wasn't enough, now we're told to handle small rodents. I think most of us would rather answer a few questions in a literature textbook. However, what Collins is offering us in terms of appreciating the shape and structure of a poem beats the most academic of exercises.

But don't just drop a mouse into the poem below. Allow yourself to *become* a mouse, wandering through stanzas and lines. How do you become a reader-mouse? Well, you picture yourself shrunk down to size, literally crawling through the poem, scampering atop the words in each line. You look for patterns to see where to go, sometimes tripping over unpredictable spaces and breaks. You enjoy traveling through the structural maze, even if you don't quite know what it means.

Ready to drop in? Come on. I'll pick you up by the tail if
I have to.

Weighing

Shaving,
I wonder how much the mirror
would weigh

with nothing in it.

I step away,
step back,
touch glass with fingertips.

Every day I do this,

looking at the face
I've earned
with countless joys and griefs.

One day I will shave and do
the ritual not knowing
it is the last time.
Every morning I am rehearsing

saying goodbye to myself.

— Neil Carpathios, from *Beyond the Bones*

In this chapter, follow me as I talk myself through the maze. I have no specific agenda in mind, no goal of leading you to the poem's "confession," as Collins would say. I just want to share my initial thoughts as I explore the cognitive and emotional impacts of the poem's architecture—modeling, I hope, a way you can approach reading your next poem.

First, I walk over "Shaving" and immediately drop off. Yep, shaving is a clean break, cutting that unwanted hair off— but for good? I then scuttle over "I wonder how much the mirror," taking a little longer to get over that line, because, well, *wondering* can linger like that. Down to "would weigh." Weigh. That's a heavy word to end on, both stanza and line. (And the title, of course, is "Weighing.") This might not be the most lighthearted poem.

Then I fall, whiskers fluttering. White space down to a single line with nothing in it. Emptiness. Sparseness. The weight of nothing—and the attention on that weight.

Next, I scamper over "I step away." I hop down at the break. I'm "away." Then "step back." Break. Quick steps back and forth as the speaker looks in that mirror, suggesting that perhaps a bit of panic is setting in. Another relatively longer line in this poem, "touch glass with fingertips," has the fluid sensation of running one's hand over a mirror's surface. I take a bit more time strolling over that line then fall into another one of those stark white spaces.

"Every day I do this." Every day. The line stands by itself because, well, this is important. The speaker conducts this shaving ceremony repeatedly. You can say it might be a central activity in his life.

Next, I bound down to "looking at the face," stepping off the edge of that ever so important image of the visage in the mirror. Even if for a split second, whatever word I find at the stop sign of a line sears my mind a bit more deeply than the others. On to "I've earned," short and to the point (he has *really* done this), then "with countless joys and griefs," the longer line, again, reflecting an idea of, well, endlessness.

Now this singleton: "One day I will shave and do." What a strange word to end a line and stanza. *Do*? It doesn't seem to hold the same power of "weigh," "mirror," "fingertips," and so on. Unless there is something significant in the doing.

Down to the last three-line stanza, "the ritual not knowing." Hop off the end of that momentary mystery. Then "it is the last time." Well, of course the last time would be at the end of a line. It's final. Then I wander over the last longer line, "Every morning I am rehearsing," wending my way through the lengthy process of practicing day in and day out, until. . .

"Saying goodbye to myself." Boom. I've reached the end, the lonely last line of farewell. The cheese is waiting for me, but, honestly, I don't know if I'm up to eating it.

Now, I'm not about to administer a "final interpretation" of this poem. I do, however, want to summarize the thoughts and feelings I experienced as a result of meandering through "Weighing" like a mouse. I went in with nothing, but found my way out of the poem with feelings of isolation, introspection, endings. Poems with different structures—longer lines, different stanza patterns and breaks, rhymes—could reflect different emotions. Wistfulness. Joy. Mania. Confusion.

The structure of a poem, the look of it on the page, does influence how we enter it, journey through it, and exit.

Images may spill into our hearts with lush emotion. Sounds may buzz in our subconscious and make us sing. But the form contains and constrains that wildness, giving us a direction for how to walk through it and breathe. This week, take the challenge of sauntering through the delightful maze of a poem. Take your time lingering over line breaks and patterns, and see how the poem comes to life. Come on, you can do it. Are you a reader—or a mouse?

Stepping Out

Take some time to wander through the mazes of the following poems. Pay attention to these twists and turns as you discover your path:

• Patterns
• Spaces
• Short lines
• Long lines
• Indented lines
• Isolated lines
• Surprising breaks
• End words
• End punctuation (or lack thereof)
• The poem's "look" on the page: smooth, jagged, even, wild, flowing, blunt

Men Who Love the Domed Heads of Old Dogs

whose hands like thick pads
polish the half-globe
from white fringed brow
to nape, those
are the men I love
who move gentle
slowly folding knees
offering homage
to the fine silk of an ear,
loving the large
nature, the teeth
that slumber behind slack lips.

Anne M. Doe Overstreet

A Graveyard

Man, looking into the sea—
taking the view from those who have as much right to it as
      you have it to yourself—
it is human nature to stand in the middle of a thing
but you cannot stand in the middle of this:
the sea has nothing to give but a well excavated grave.
The firs stand in a procession—each with an emerald
      turkey-foot at the top—
reserved as their contours, saying nothing;
repression, however, is not the most obvious characteristic
      of the sea;
the sea is a collector, quick to return a rapacious look.
There are others besides you who have worn that look—
whose expression is no longer a protest; the fish no longer
      investigate them
for their bones have not lasted;
men lower nets, unconscious of the fact that they are
      desecrating a grave,
and row quickly away—the blades of the oars
moving together like the feet of water-spiders as if
      there were no such thing as death.
The wrinkles progress upon themselves in a phalanx—
      beautiful under networks of foam,
and fade breathlessly while the sea rustles in and out
      of the seaweed;
the birds swim through the air at top speed, emitting
      cat-calls as heretofore—
the tortoise-shell scourges about the feet of the cliffs,

in motion beneath them
and the ocean, under the pulsation of light-houses and noise
    of bell-buoys,
advances as usual, looking as if it were not that ocean in
    which dropped things are bound to
sink—
in which if they turn and twist, it is neither with volition nor
    consciousness.

Marianne Moore

Life in a Love

Escape me?
Never—
Beloved!
While I am, and you are you,
  So long as the world contains us both,
  Me the loving and you the loth,
While the one eludes, must the other pursue.
My life is a fault at last, I fear:
 It seems too much like a fate, indeed!
 Though I do my best I shall scarce succeed.
But what if I fail of my purpose here?
It is but to keep the nerves at strain,
  To dry one's eyes and laugh at a fall,
And baffled, get up to begin again,—
  So the chase takes up one's life, that's all.
While, look but once from your farthest bound,
  At me so deep in the dust and dark,
No sooner the old hope drops to ground
  Than a new one, straight to the selfsame mark,
I shape me—
Ever
Removed!

Robert Browning

To the Swimmer

Now as I watch you, strong of arm and endurance, battling
  and struggling
With the waves that rush against you, ever with invincible
  strength returning
Into my heart, grown each day more tranquil and peaceful,
  comes a fierce longing
Of mind and soul that will not be appeased until, like you,
  I breast yon deep and boundless expanse of blue.

With an outward stroke of power intense your mighty
  arm goes forth,
Cleaving its way through waters that rise and roll, ever a
  ceaseless vigil keeping
Over the treasures beneath.

My heart goes out to you of dauntless courage and
  spirit indomitable,
And though my lips would speak, my spirit forbids me
  to ask,
"Is your heart as true as your arm?"

Countee Cullen

Blessing

This world is little
more than a single
leaf
dangling
on a bare branch,
trembling
in the wind,

but, look,
how the late afternoon
light
catches the green.

Benjamin Myers

Mnemosyne

It's autumn in the country I remember.

How warm a wind blew here about the ways!
And shadows on the hillside lay to slumber
During the long sun-sweetened summer-days.

It's cold abroad the country I remember.

The swallows veering skimmed the golden grain
At midday with a wing aslant and limber;
And yellow cattle browsed upon the plain.

It's empty down the country I remember.

I had a sister lovely in my sight:
Her hair was dark, her eyes were very sombre;
We sang together in the woods at night.

It's lonely in the country I remember.

The babble of our children fills my ears,
And on our hearth I stare the perished ember
To flames that show all starry thro' my tears.

It's dark about the country I remember.

There are the mountains where I lived. The path
Is slushed with cattle-tracks and fallen timber,
The stumps are twisted by the tempests' wrath.

But that I knew these places are my own,
I'd ask how came such wretchedness to cumber
The earth, and I to people it alone.

It rains across the country I remember.

Trumbull Stickney

I Am a Parcel of Vain Strivings Tied

I am a parcel of vain strivings tied
      By a chance bond together,
Dangling this way and that, their links
      Were made so loose and wide,
           Methinks,
      For milder weather.

A bunch of violets without their roots,
      And sorrel intermixed,
Encircled by a wisp of straw
      Once coiled about their shoots,
           The law
      By which I'm fixed.

A nosegay which Time clutched from out
      Those fair Elysian fields,
With weeds and broken stems, in haste,
      Doth make the rabble rout
           That waste
      The day he yields.

And here I bloom for a short hour unseen,
      Drinking my juices up,
With no root in the land
      To keep my branches green,
           But stand
      In a bare cup.

Some tender buds were left upon my stem
        In mimicry of life,
But ah! the children will not know,
        Till time has withered them,
                The woe
        With which they're rife.

But now I see I was not plucked for naught,
        And after in life's vase
Of glass set while I might survive,
        But by a kind hand brought
                Alive
        To a strange place.

That stock thus thinned will soon redeem its hours,
        And by another year,
Such as God knows, with freer air,
        More fruits and fairer flowers
                Will bear,
        While I droop here.

Henry David Thoreau

No More Same Old Silly Love Songs

When the radio in my car broke I started to notice the trees.
I began to stop exaggerating the color of leaves,
how their reds and oranges needed no wordy embellishment.

I started to open the window and smell the wet pavement.

after morning rain. Crows on the phone line,
their blackness and stubborn dignity. I even noticed my hands

gripping the wheel, the small dark hairs, the skin,
the knuckles and the perfect blue veins.

Neil Carpathios

Li Po

1

Li Po knew
the fecund trees
full of blossoms,
the tea bushes
flush with leaves,
sweet scent rising
from snow-petaled earth,
spears rolled—or broken—
between fingers and thumb

2

Every morning
I am Li Po,
if only I hear
the expectant cup

3

And if the porcelain overturns,
what then?

4

the snow-petaled earth
the snow-petaled earth

L.L. Barkat

4

Feeling for the Switch: That Aha! Moment

So far, we've explored how we can spend time with imagery, sound, and structure to help us fall in love with poetry. In this chapter, things get even a little more…adventurous.

After exhorting us to hold a poem up to the light, press our ear to its hive, and drop a mouse into its lines, Collins now tells us to

> …walk inside the poem's room
> and feel the walls for a light switch.

Hold on a moment. Throughout this book, we've been talking about how to enjoy a poem without necessarily finding its one "correct answer," how to love poetry without, as Collins says later in his poem, *torturing a confession out of it*. But isn't the metaphor here pretty clear? Finding a switch, which is on one specific, permanent place on the wall, implies that readers are just one strategic flick away from finding out what a poem *really* means. Billy, are you contradicting yourself here? Did you just sabotage this book?

I don't think so.

Consider these words from a recent conversation I had with poet and editor Marci Rae Johnson: "*Seeing the light* is not a moment of completely understanding meaning, but a moment when you connect with a poem and fall in love with it."

She then invoked these famous words from Emily Dickinson: "If I feel physically as if the top of my head were taken off, I know *that* is poetry. [This is] the only way I know it. Is there any other way?" Sometimes you see the light, or, more violently, lose your cranium. But no matter the severity of the moment, you read poetry in hopes of a *moment*. And I believe if you read with an open mind, you'll find it. The light may switch on before you even completely grasp the whole poem, but that dawning will make you want to read it again and again, even motivate you to increase your understanding of a seemingly difficult poem.

Let's look at this light switch metaphor a little more closely.

Imagine you're staying in a guest room at an unfamiliar house. In the middle of the night, you realize you've forgotten to take your vitamins, so you stumble out of bed to find the light. (This happened to me when I stayed in the house of a woman I had just met.)

You move your hands along the wall to feel for the switch. When you turn on the light, you take a moment to look more closely at this strange place. You feel instantly drawn toward what you see—pictures of your host's extended family, flowering cacti, cat paintings—but you don't necessarily know the stories behind them, and you definitely don't know what's in the drawers or under the bed.

But if you are drawn to the room, you will want to spend more time looking, even snooping, around. You'll start to find clues and make connections. From the images, you'll discern the family's priorities and tastes, piecing together their history. You'll start to identify and even love strange sounds, like the honey locust branch brushing against the window. You'll start to learn this room's path, even in the dark. And you're pretty sure you'll want to come back and stay again.

Here's a poetry "room" I visited with that sense of interest and curiosity:

Want Me

Lemons crystallized in sugar, glistening
on a blue-glazed plate. The rarest volume
bound in blood leather. A silk carpet
woven so finely you can't push a needle through,
that from one edge is the silver of a leaf
underwater, and from the other bleu lumière,
first frost on the cornflowers. A duet for cello
and woodsmoke, violin and icicle. Tangle of
black hair steeped in sandalwood, jasmine,
bergamot and vetiver and jewelled
with pomegranate seeds. Panther's broad tongue
soothing hunt-bruised paws. Eyelids of ribbonsnakes.
Taut skin of a lavender crème brûlée. Split
vanilla pods swollen with bourbon. A luna
moth's wings, enormous, celadon, trembling.

— Melissa Stein, from *Rough Honey*

Now, this is one of the most luscious poems I've read (talk about image and sound!). I love every word, every sensual picture. But when I feel the walls of the poem, where do I find the switch?

For me, it's the phrase "Eyelids of ribbonsnakes." Every time I read the poem, that's the sentence that lights up the entire opulent room, giving me goose bumps. After that important gut reaction, I look a little more closely, applying what I've been exploring with image, sound, and line. I see something that can barely be seen. A miniature flicker. A fleeting face in the leaves. I hear those mysterious "s" sounds that remind me of secrets, whispers—and snakes. I stop at the end of the line, where the ribbonsnake also comes to a stop. Or disappears? Is that a good disappearing, since most people hate snakes? Or a bad one, since, well, the little blinking guy is gone? (For the record, I think ribbonsnakes are adorable.)

This is what lights up the rest of the poem. Suddenly everywhere I see mystery and desire, life and longing, deliciousness and pain. I read the poem again and again. The little snake has turned on the switch, and now everything is pulsing and glowing.

How does the snake light up the poem for you? Or if not, how does another line, image, or simply a word, turn on the switch? Stay in this poem's room awhile. Be my guest. You might even get a coupon for your next night's stay.

Stepping Out

Pay a visit to the following poetry "rooms," keeping a spirit of wonder and exploration. As you feel for the light switches, use these questions as travel tips:

• At what point do you feel an instant "gut" connection to the poem?

• What words, images, or lines do you fall in love with, even if you don't "get" them?

• What parts do you find yourself reading over and over again?

• What parts "light up" the poem for you?

• In what ways do those words connect with you the most? Image? Sound? Personal connections? Memories?

• How do those words light up the rest of the poem?

Back Yard

Shine on, O moon of summer.
Shine to the leaves of grass, catalpa and oak,
All silver under your rain to-night.

An Italian boy is sending songs to you to-night from
      an accordion.
A Polish boy is out with his best girl; they marry next month;
    to-night they are throwing you kisses.

An old man next door is dreaming over a sheen that sits in a
    cherry tree in his back yard.

The clocks say I must go—I stay here sitting on the back
      porch drinking
    white thoughts you rain down.

    Shine on, O moon,
Shake out more and more silver changes.

Carl Sandburg

Body in Motion

Sinew, charge, and light—
muscle etching a concourse of air,
heat and flutter
thrum of pump house,
or pop of ligaments
snapping shut.
So quiet the fabric of skin,
taut, slack then taut again.
Flex and stretch with single purpose,
gauge of weight and distribution.
Placement of form becoming new,
as in never accomplished before,
as in a position to be named later.
Sublime, the arc of breath:
ether of air, atom, matter—
particles colluding in space.

Scott Edward Anderson

Sonnets from the Portuguese 5:
I lift my heavy heart up solemnly

I lift my heavy heart up solemnly,
As once Electra her sepulchral urn,
And, looking in thine eyes, I overturn
The ashes at thy feet. Behold and see
What a great heap of grief lay hid in me,
And how the red wild sparkles dimly burn
Through the ashen greyness. If thy foot in scorn
Could tread them out to darkness utterly,
It might be well perhaps. But if instead
Thou wait beside me for the wind to blow
The grey dust up, . . . those laurels on thine head,
O My beloved, will not shield thee so,
That none of all the fires shall scorch and shred
The hair beneath. Stand further off then! Go.

Elizabeth Barrett Browning

The Gravity Soundtrack

Even now, grounded, a song scrap
drifting out a third-floor window
slips through the bare oak limbs,
firing memory: the skin on my back,
shag carpet, a tank top. A car door
slams and I stop. Were we as thin

and quiet as I see us now through
my Vaseline lens? Me with long hair,
sprawled on your floor, cheap walls,
pulsing with bass. Your wild head
an inch away, eyes on the ceiling,
painting in your mind. We were

scared, fatherless kids who couldn't
name the men we loved. We were
something like veal. Outside, a boy
snapped firecrackers, round after
round in the dry August night. You

cranked the volume. We wanted to
see how long we could hold our breath,
waiting, waiting, for spots in our eyes,
the burn in our bellies, for the slow
false rise from the floor, the lifting,
the dizziness that felt like floating.

Erin Keane

Dreamers

Soldiers are citizens of death's grey land,
Drawing no dividend from time's to-morrows.
In the great hour of destiny they stand,
Each with his feuds, and jealousies, and sorrows.
Soldiers are sworn to action; they must win
Some flaming, fatal climax with their lives.
Soldiers are dreamers; when the guns begin
They think of firelit homes, clean beds and wives.

I see them in foul dug-outs, gnawed by rats,
And in the ruined trenches, lashed with rain,
Dreaming of things they did with balls and bats,
And mocked by hopeless longing to regain
Bank-holidays, and picture shows, and spats,
And going to the office in the train.

Siegfried Sassoon

One Life

I don't know when I stopped believing in heaven,
or if I do. Maybe I just stopped receiving heaven.

The sun rose. I climbed into the pines' brittle
crowns. You could say I was retrieving heaven.

Not a place or a time, but blindness to everything
but one light, pulsing, pleasing: heaven.

We married in September. Everyone was still
wearing their summer shirts, sleeves of heaven.

It was white, there was a bend, and the car
spun. It was then I prayed, pleading with heaven.

When he goes limp, lie him down on the gurney,
Mom. Oxygen mask, breathing heaven.

The hospital shines, our son flies in and out.
The snow falls hard, relieving heaven.

He loves the colors of planets. I teach him
their lifelessness: beautiful, deceiving heaven.

I don't know who is buried beneath me
but I hear her break as I am leaving heaven.

How can you cry for one ruined life, Maria,
when you could be grieving for heaven?

Maria Hummel

My Life with a Gardener

The screen door firecrackers closed.
I find her at the sundry drawer
prowling for twine. I'm nothing
she sees. There's a tornado
in her hair, her face is streaked
with dirt like markings applied
before the rituals of drums.
I've watched her shadow break free
and tend the next row of corn.
I understand this eagerness
as fully as I can speak for the ocean.
I say water is behind everything,
a blue dictator, say waves
are obsessed with their one word
but have no idea what that word is.
Her hands enter soil like needles
making the promise of a dress
from cloth. In December she begins
smelling lilacs, by February
she sees the holes
peppers burn through snow. I see her,
she's the last green thing I need.
When finally she's pushed inside
by the rude hands of dusk,
I set down my life for her skin,
taught all day how to smell
like the sun, and the hundred

directions of her hair, and eyes
that look through me to flowers
that only open their mouths
to speak with the moon.

Bob Hicok

The Dress of Self-Generating Sorrow

When it was fully ripe
high in the branches,
the women gathered.

How long had they been waiting?

Since before
anyone's grandmother could remember,
though mustn't the tree
have been a sapling once?

The vigilance.
The constant tending.
The bearing of water to the roots
in times of little water.

And now, harvest—
this gown whose stains and ruptures
had arisen from within its very threads,
or perhaps anticipated them,

lacework growing around each torn place
like flesh around a constellation of lesions.

But also ripe now,
the question:

who would be the one
to bring it down?

Claire Bateman

Women

Women have no wilderness in them,
They are provident instead,
Content in the tight hot cell of their hearts
To eat dusty bread.

They do not see cattle cropping red winter grass,
They do not hear
Snow water going down under culverts
Shallow and clear.

They wait, when they should turn to journeys,
They stiffen, when they should bend.
They use against themselves that benevolence
To which no man is friend.

They cannot think of so many crops to a field
Or of clean wood cleft by an axe.
Their love is an eager meaninglessness
Too tense, or too lax.

They hear in every whisper that speaks to them
A shout and a cry.
As like as not, when they take life over their door-sills
They should let it go by.

Louise Bogan

5

Skiing Across a Poem:
Reading without the Poet's Help

Throughout our field guide, I've been pretty much ignoring the poets themselves. Now I'll do it again. This time, totally, unequivocally, on purpose.

It's not that I don't like poets. I'm a poet, and some of my best friends are poets. We tend to appreciate good chocolate and colorful scarves. But when it comes to enjoying a poem, well, the poet rarely matters. Consider Collins's words:

> I want them to waterski
> across the surface of a poem
> waving at the author's name on the shore.

Is a writer's life completely irrelevant to understanding a text? As writing coach and editor Ann Kroeker points out, "Sometimes knowing about a writer's life is good…so that a student doesn't read, say, *The Scarlet Letter*, thinking it was written at the time of the Puritans." Yes, it helps to know an author's time period so we don't, going along with the water-skiing metaphor, completely miss the boat. And we can gain insight into poems when delving into the fascinating lives of Emily Dickinson and Sylvia Plath. But when it comes to the sheer wind-blowing-in-the-hair fun of reading a poem—yes, skiing across the glorious blue surface without giving a lick for the

molecular structures and creatures beneath you—you don't
need a biography. "Hey," you yell to the poet, waving from
your skis. "Great poem!" Then you go back to it.

Consider my experience with this poem:

SRV in the Parking Lot at the Quick Stop

No traffic,
light coming up
with the radio—
Lenny's here, really here.
Do you cry
when you play her,
where the fret moves into the music box
I dance inside,
sometimes I risk it driving—
bow my head and shake
where the clear notes sound tenor up the neck,
bass in a tin can like a kick
oh my!
Margarine for my sweetheart, butter me—
whiskey's too early, but those cigarettes
sleep in my heart like a snare vibrating
in the red rising sky like it's all I've got left.

Here now, people come and go,
Lenny loud low, lingering me in the parking lot—
I can't leave you like this radio,
staring into the space behind the world,

fingers walking like these vagabond birds—
not for sweet love or even neat coffee.

— Richard Maxson

What sheer musical delight! Our practices from this series—allowing images to stun and connect us ("fingers walking like these vagabond birds"), reveling in sound ("bass in a tin can like a kick"), running nimbly over lines and their breaks (this poem is a fretboard of dashes), and feeling for a light-switch moment ("Here now, people come and go")—have me dancing inside this poem's music box.

And you know, I don't know a thing about Richard Maxson, the author. I didn't even know SRV was the common nickname for Stevie Ray Vaughan until I did a Google search.

Am I contradicting myself by looking up this information?

Well, if I had set out to conduct in-depth research before even reading the poem, yes. If I had read the poem with preconceived notions about the poet and Stevie Ray Vaughan himself, I may have stalled in the water, analyzing the lines in context of my newfound knowledge, breaking the momentum of my initial, gliding joy over the waves.

Someone with that blues background would have integrated it naturally, probably unconsciously, on the initial read. I didn't, but now that I revisit the poem after listening to "Texas Flood," "I'm Crying," and "Lenny," I appreciate the author's rhythm and soul even more. My experience is enriched, not tripped up.

Ann Kroeker again:

> The poem must stand alone as its own thing;
> it should provide enough support that a
> reader can cruise comfortably all the way
> across the poem without sinking into re-
> search—and assumptions—about its author.
> The more the reader gets bogged down with
> information about the author, the more
> stretchy and stringy and sloshy the lines of
> the poem get; the poem's own meaning and
> identity get jumbled up with the history and
> identity of the author.

Getting bogged down in research not only impacts those initial
readings of poems; it often discourages potential poetry readers from strapping on the skis in the first place. I have met
many people who say they would read poetry if only they
knew more about it, if only they understood more about the
poets themselves. How freeing to know you can enjoy a
poem—yes, even "just" its glittering surface—without receiving a full literary education first. The more you read and enjoy
the poetry, the more the understanding and information will
come as a natural outgrowth of committing yourself to the
poems themselves, the most important thing.

"SRV in the Parking Lot of the Quick Stop" clearly stands
alone as "its own thing." I don't need to know anything about
Richard Maxson in order to love his poem—although I do
hope to know him and his work better as his own exuberant
songs play on.

Stepping Out

Some of the following poems may seem difficult to fully "get" without conducting initial background research on the poets, their time periods, or historical references in the poems.

However, before doing any outside reading, enjoy gliding over a poem without prior assumptions or interruptions. Take your time. Appreciate it for what it has to offer you: pictures, sounds, lines, and light switches.

After allowing the poem to stand as "its own thing," feel free to research. Does the new information enrich your experience? Why or why not?

The Daughter

We said she was a negative image of me because of
     her lightness.
She's light and also passage, the glory in my cortex.
Daughter, where did you get all that goddess?
Her eyes are Neruda's two dark pools at twilight.
Sometimes she's a stranger in my home because I hadn't
     imagined her.
Who will her daughter be?
She and I are the gradual ebb of my mother's darkness.
I unfurl the ribbon of her life, and it's a smooth long hallway,
doors flung open.
Her surface is a deflection is why.
Harm on her, harm on us all.
Inside her, my grit and timbre, my reckless.

Carmen Giménez Smith

Bright Star

Bright star, would I were stedfast as thou art—
    Not in lone splendour hung aloft the night
And watching, with eternal lids apart,
    Like nature's patient, sleepless Eremite,
The moving waters at their priestlike task
    Of pure ablution round earth's human shores,
Or gazing on the new soft-fallen mask
    Of snow upon the mountains and the moors—
No—yet still stedfast, still unchangeable,
    Pillow'd upon my fair love's ripening breast,
To feel for ever its soft fall and swell,
    Awake for ever in a sweet unrest,
Still, still to hear her tender-taken breath,
And so live ever—or else swoon to death.

John Keats

Toussaint L'Ouverture

To those fair isles where crimson sunsets burn,
We send a backward glance to gaze on thee,
Brave Toussaint! thou was surely born to be
A hero; thy proud spirit could but spurn
Each outrage on the race. Couldst thou unlearn
The lessons taught by instinct? Nay! and we
Who share the zeal that would make all men free,
Must e'en with pride unto thy life-work turn.
Soul-dignity was thine and purest aim;
And ah! how sad that thou wast left to mourn
In chains 'neath alien skies. On him, shame! shame!
That mighty conqueror who dared to claim
The right to bind thee. Him we heap with scorn,
And noble patriot! guard with love thy name.

Henrietta Cordelia Ray

The Keepsake

Love fades away, the keepsake she left me is these children,
    three or four.
I eat, I sleep … it's all the same today as yesterday.
The clock strikes one at midnight,
I spring up, I straighten a quilt over the sleeping children,
    by my side.

Love faded away, true love will return to me never again …
Love faded away before I grasped her tight.
But what's that?—the clock goes on striking.

Love faded away, the rats in the ceiling gnaw a pillar,
My life too is bitten by a tough chap called Time ….
There's tomorrow, there's tomorrow, things will be done
    tomorrow …
I ask myself, what's that tomorrow you speak about?

The houses stand like the teeth of a comb,
I build in one of them my own nest,
And gaze at the keepsake Love left me.

Yone Noguchi

The Poster Girl's Defence

It was an Artless Poster Girl pinned up against my wall,
She was tremendous ugly, she was exceeding tall;
I was gazing at her idly, and I think I must have slept,
For that poster maiden lifted up her poster voice, and wept.

She said between her poster sobs, 'I think it's rather rough
To be jeered and fleered and flouted, and I've stood it long
      enough;
I'm tired of being quoted as a Fright and Fad and Freak,
And I take this opportunity my poster mind to speak.

'Although my hair is carmine and my nose is edged with blue,
Although my style is splashy and my shade effects are few,
Although I'm out of drawing and my back hair is a show,
Yet I haven't half the whimseys of the maidens that you
      know.

'I never keep you waiting while I prink before the glass,
I never talk such twaddle as that little Dawson lass,
I never paint on china, nor erotic novels write,
And I never have recited "Curfew must not ring tonight".

'I don't rave over Ibsen, I never, never flirt,
I never wear a shirt waist with a disconnected skirt;
I never speak in public on "The Suffrage", or "The Race",
I never talk while playing whist, or trump my partner's ace.'

I said: 'O artless Poster Girl, you're in the right of it,
You are a joy forever, though a thing of beauty, nit!'
And from her madder eyebrows to her utmost purple swirl,
Against all captious critics I'll defend the Poster Girl.

Carolyn Wells

Kashmiri Song

Pale hands I loved beside the Shalimar,
　　Where are you now? Who lies beneath your spell?
Whom do you lead on Rapture's roadway, far,
　　Before you agonise them in farewell?

Oh, pale dispensers of my Joys and Pains,
　　Holding the doors of Heaven and of Hell,
How the hot blood rushed wildly through the veins,
　　Beneath your touch, until you waved farewell.

Pale hands, pink tipped, like Lotus buds that float
　　On those cool waters where we used to dwell,
I would have rather felt you round my throat,
　　Crushing out life, than waving me farewell!

Laurence Hope

Aunt Helen

Miss Helen Slingsby was my maiden aunt,
And lived in a small house near a fashionable square
Cared for by servants to the number of four.
Now when she died there was silence in heaven
And silence at her end of the street.
The shutters were drawn and the undertaker wiped his feet —
He was aware that this sort of thing had occurred before.
The dogs were handsomely provided for,
But shortly afterwards the parrot died too.
The Dresden clock continued ticking on the mantelpiece,
And the footman sat upon the dining-table
Holding the second housemaid on his knees —
Who had always been so careful while her mistress lived.

T. S. Eliot

Cousin Nancy

Miss Nancy Ellicott
Strode across the hills and broke them,
Rode across the hills and broke them —
The barren New England hills —
Riding to hounds
Over the cow-pasture.

Miss Nancy Ellicott smoked
And danced all the modern dances;
And her aunts were not quite sure how they felt about it,
But they knew that it was modern.

Upon the glazen shelves kept watch
Matthew and Waldo, guardians of the faith,
The army of unalterable law.

T. S. Eliot

Portrait by Matisse

Yours is a music
of morning sunlight:

a shaft of wheat,
also the mood of a paling moon,
the blue of the town madam on Christmas Eve.

You, poet of crayons and cutouts and glue,
dance me through October dew:

color it champagne
lighter than swallows in flight,
your thought the rest.

I slip onto your easel dressed in the scarlets
of mad words and love's open sores.

Even when you set me against a background
not exactly white, men smile at me,

The laughter in your hands contagious after all.

Maureen Doallas

Your Voice

Amazing the mood it's put me in.
And the sky's tint at this hour—out
on my own, occasional hum or zip

of a car, August the summer month
half the city splashes about
the Mediterranean, or north:

the beach at Donostia a jewel
—its Paseo the lip of a shell to walk.
It's hearing you what really pulls

me in, soft this interior punch,
recalling the sheen of your brow—we'd talk
with our limbs, the Liffey below, have lunch...

Re-lived this evening on the phone;
the pitch of your Dublin tone.

Madrid

Francisco Aragón

There may be Chaos still around the World

There may be chaos still around the world,
This little world that in my thinking lies;
For mine own bosom is the paradise
Where all my life's fair visions are unfurled.
Within my nature's shell I slumber curled,
Unmindful of the changing outer skies,
Where now, perchance, some new-born Eros flies,
Or some old Cronos from his throne is hurled.
I heed them not; or if the subtle night
Haunt me with deities I never saw,
I soon mine eyelid's drowsy curtain draw
To hide their myriad faces from my sight.
They threat in vain; the whirlwind cannot awe
A happy snow-flake dancing in the flaw.

George Santayana

6

True Confessions: Let a Poem Be

We have reignited—or ignited for the first time—a love for poetry by simply being with poems. Using Billy Collins as our spirit guide, we've learned how to dwell within the possibility of image, sound, line, epiphany, and freedom.

Now, of course, it's time to discuss confession and torture. I mean, it wouldn't be a real learning experience without that, right?

Consider the last two stanzas of "Introduction to Poetry":

> But all they want to do
> is tie the poem to a chair with rope
> and torture a confession out of it.
>
> They begin beating it with a hose
> to find out what it really means.

The first three lines conjure up the classic image of the suspect in a room with a concrete floor, tied to a chair with a single bright bulb over his head. Here the poem is powerless, bound with no hope of movement. In a torture situation, the suspect often gives up the "truth" by acquiescing or creating new falsehoods to escape the pain. Torture leads to the desire for a quick end, and desperate utterances are treated as hard fact.

Sound familiar? Ever been in a classroom where student and instructor were so fatigued or near the bell that they drove toward the "answer" just to get the darn thing done? As a high school teacher, I'd gotten to that point: "Guys, Daisy's green light on the dock represents an unquenchable desire for the American Dream's mythology of money and happiness, okay? See you tomorrow." Even as we read poetry in solitude, we can find ourselves rushing toward a conclusion. There are so many poems and posts and emails to read and so many more demands for our time.

Dwelling with a poem requires more attention, love, imagination and freedom than just getting the job done. And, of course, a poem doesn't have an answer anyway, as I've been discussing throughout this guide. It offers an experience. Christian Wiman in his book *My Bright Abyss* says, "A poem, if it's a real one, in some fundamental sense means no more and no less than the moment of its singular music and lightning insight; it is its own code to its own absolute and irreducible clarity."

Singular music and lightning insight. A poem is a poem is a poem. Let's read it over and over—not as a form of torture but as an expression of love for the poem and ourselves.

For the last two lines of this poem, I had to do a little research. What's the deal with the hose? Before the Supreme Court put an end to "third degree" back room interrogations, police often beat suspects with rubber hoses that did not leave marks on the skin. The beatings, however, were excruciating, and while I believe poems are resilient, they can undergo some duress that puts psychological distance between them and their readers. Again, Wiman writes: "The trouble comes when the effort to name and know an experience replaces the experience itself. Just as we seem to have grasped every level of meaning in a poem, the private and silent power that compelled us in the first place drains right out of it." Just as torturing a person can degrade his humanity, torturing a poem can drain it of its power.

It's not that reading a poem assiduously is wrong, that analyzing it, even, is the same as beating it to death. It's the attitude of facing a poem as an obstacle to be overcome or a puzzle to be solved that siphons off its magic. After torturing a poem a few times, then, many readers start to see all poems as automatic suspects, committing the crime of being poems. How many of us have shaken our heads at poems? "Too confusing. Too much work. Too smart for someone like me."

Really?

Let's review our journey by reading Collins's poem again:

Introduction to Poetry

I ask them to take a poem
and hold it up to the light
like a color slide

Poem, imagery is your lifeblood. I will read to see *before anything else. I will let your colors and shapes light up the page, flipping through them again and again before I even know what they mean.*

or press an ear against its hive.

I will listen to the sounds buzzing around in your world—consonants knocking together, the viscous liquid of your vowels. I will read you aloud and taste your delicious words in my mouth long before I know what they mean.

> I say drop a mouse into a poem
> and watch him probe his way out,

I will become the mouse, the wanderer through your stanzas and lines. I will look for patterns to see where to go, sometimes tripping on unpredictable spaces and breaks. I will enjoy traveling through your structural maze…even if I don't know what it means.

> or walk inside the poem's room
> and feel the walls for a light switch.

Poem, after spending time delighting in your pictures, sounds, and shape, I will go back in your room to feel—yes, this is my memory and gut working now—my way to some illumination. Not an answer, but a new light, a new way to see. Poem, you don't need to mean *to be meaningful.*

> I want them to waterski
> across the surface of a poem
> waving at the author's name on the shore.

But wait—let's not stop having fun. When I get too bogged down, too intent on finding the perfect switch, I'll read you again for the thrill. The author is asleep on her beach towel by now, and you are on your own. It's just between you and me. What we mean together.

> But all they want to do

is tie the poem to a chair with rope
and torture a confession out of it.

I will let you be free, poem. I promise. Once I force you to give the final word, it goes on record and we can never go back again. You know what I mean.

They begin beating it with a hose
to find out what it really means.

It's not about beating you to death. But it's also not about being simplistic. It's about giving you the time to work in my heart and mind, about opening both of us to the possibilities that change with every new reading. Every new meaning.

Stepping Out

Remember, a poem is not a problem to solve, but an experience to live. Read these last poems with as much attention, love, fun, and freedom as you can muster. Walk the fields. Enjoy.

Mowing at Dusk

Grass pours from the mower's side,
glitters in the last light.
There's satisfaction
in small tasks,
drifting in neutral,
the turf reduced
to simple geometry,
the blade cutting
a clean path,
a swath of green,
patterns of surf.
I could drown in this noise
that pours over me;
I glitter in the last light.
Scents of rose and tarragon
hang starry in the night air
where the catcher brushes them.
Fireflies wink on and on,
signals from the shore.
Landlocked in Pennsylvania,
my kitchen light beacons.
I rudder home in the salty dark.

Barbara Crooker

The Waves

It is likely that the waves
are what you heard last night
or last week or month
and have forgotten
though they woke you.
No matter you live landlocked.
I've heard them too;
so has my wife.
(Not the baby;
they don't seem to hear
the waves.)
You and I, though, we're fated for this,
to wake again to the crash. Only
next time it will come from inside us.

Daniel Bowman, Jr.

Gathered

The day rose with shivered light, bees braiding a path
before his eye had even opened.

Rose the woman, resonant as a struck cello.

The beekeeper entered his kitchen among the crumbs
from dinner, all taste a light on the tongue.

Blind, but it was only light, bees blurring past, softening
into butter.

He stepped outside the door, entered the patterns among
fireweed, sourwood, goldenrod.

Rose on the balls of his feet, raised his face toward heat
and hum, placed a hand on the hive wall. Found himself

spilled back into the embrace of the woman. Entered
the sound everywhere, gathered like glass, boozy with gold.

Anne M. Doe Overstreet

Winter Stars

I went out at night alone;
 The young blood flowing beyond the sea
Seemed to have drenched my spirit's wings—
 I bore my sorrow heavily.

But when I lifted up my head
 From shadows shaken on the snow,
I saw Orion in the east
 Burn steadily as long ago.

From windows in my father's house,
 Dreaming my dreams on winter nights,
I watched Orion as a girl
 Above another city's lights.

Years go, dreams go, and youth goes too,
 The world's heart breaks beneath its wars,
All things are changed, save in the east
 The faithful beauty of the stars.

Sara Teasdale

Upon Julia's Clothes

Whenas in silks my Julia goes,
Then, then (methinks) how sweetly flows
That liquefaction of her clothes.

Next, when I cast mine eyes, and see
That brave vibration each way free,
O how that glittering taketh me!

Robert Herrick

Phoenix

As if my mother feared he might
regenerate we scattered him through
three states—a few handfuls among
the ash and birch along the trails he ran,
wind spitting him back into our faces—
a small box of my father strafed
from the car along an Indiana field—
then at dusk a ceremonial loosing
of him across a green bed of waves.
Last summer, drought burned the sky
to bright bone and I walked a field,
a beach, the weeded path through dry
woods, collected him in my beard, gray
ash in the creases of my face, my hands.

David Wright

Erithracus Rubecula

At evening, the small bird comes
on a whirr of wings to its chosen home.

It polishes chortle notes in the depth of its throat,
behind closed beak. It sings to itself alone,

the whole of its being is singing. And I must stand
and wait, the tips of my toes thrusting roots

between paving flags, my outstretched arm
clad in a sleeve of bark ridged with longing.

Jill Eulalie Dawson

Tutto è Sciolto

A birdless heaven, sea-dusk and a star
Sad in the west;
And thou, poor heart, love's image, fond and far,
Rememberest:

Her silent eyes and her soft foam-white brow
And fragrant hair,
Falling as in the silence falleth now
Dusk from the air.

Ah, why wilt thou remember these, or why,
Poor heart, repine,
If the sweet love she yielded with a sigh
Was never thine?

James Joyce

Notes

The Reading Soul

page 13   "one precious and wild life": Mary Oliver, *New and Selected Poems*, "The Summer Day" (Boston: Beacon Press, 1992), p. 94.

Chapter 1

page 14   "a specially mounted individual transparency intended for projection onto a screen using a slide projector": (Accessed online at Wikipedia.com, "Reversal Film," June 2013). <http://en.wikipedia.org/wiki/Reversal_film>

Chapter 2

page 33   "maybe it's that sound doesn't happen in the mind": Benjamin Myers, personal correspondence, June 27, 2013.

Chapter 4

page 64   "*Seeing the light* is not a moment of completely understanding": Marci Rae Johnson, personal interview, July 17, 2013.

page 65   "If I feel physically as if the top of my head were taken off": (Accessed online at Emily Dickinson Museum: The Homestead and Evergreens, "Emily Dickinson: The Later Years

(1865-1886)," December 2013.)
<http://www.emilydickinsonmuseum.org/later
_years>

Chapter 5

page 81   "Sometimes knowing about a writer's life is good... doesn't read, say, *The Scarlet Letter*, thinking it was written at the time of the Puritans": Ann Kroeker, personal correspondence, July 24, 2013.

page 84   "The poem must stand alone as its own thing": Ann Kroeker, personal correspondence, July 24, 2013.

Chapter 6

page 99   "A poem, if it's a real one, in some fundamental sense means": Christian Wiman, *My Bright Abyss: Meditation of a Modern Believer* (New York: Farrar, Straus and Giroux, 2013), p. 87.

page 99   Before the Supreme Court put an end to "third degree" back room interrogations: "How Police Interrogation Works," Julia Layton (Accessed online at howstuffworks.com July 2013). <http://www.howstuffworks.com/police-interrogation.htm>

page 100   "The trouble comes when the effort to name and know": Christian Wiman, Ibid, p. 87.

Permissions

All poems in this book are reprinted with permission or are within the public domain. We are grateful to the authors, editors, and publishers who have given us permission to include these poems in this anthology.

Kelli Russell Agodon, "The Moon is a Comma, a Pause in the Sky," from *Virginia Quarterly Review*, 2013. Reprinted with permission of the author.

Scott Edward Anderson, "Body in Motion," from *Fallow Field*, Aldrich Press, 2013. Reprinted with permission of the author.

Francisco Aragón, "Your Voice," from *Glow of Our Sweat*, Scapegoat Press, 2010. Reprinted with permission of the author.

L.L. Barkat, "Petit à Petit L'Oiseau Fait Son Nid," from *The Novelist*, T. S. Poetry Press, 2012. Reprinted with permission of T. S. Poetry Press.

L.L. Barkat, "Li Po," from *The Novelist*, T. S. Poetry Press, 2012. Reprinted with permission of T. S. Poetry Press.

Claire Bateman, "It is the Wings," originally appearing as part of "To Night," *Alabama Literary Review* 19.1 (Fall 2010): 56. Reprinted with permission of the author.

Claire Bateman, "The Dress of Self-Generating Sorrow," from the e-chapbook "The Waterbird." *Mudlark: An Electronic Journal of Poetry & Poetics*. (December 2011): http://www.unf.edu/mudlark/mudlark44/con

tents_bateman.html. Reprinted with permission of the author.

Daniel Bowman, Jr., "The Waves," from *The Plum Tree in Leatherstocking Country*, Virtual Artists Collective, 2012. Reprinted with permission of the author.

Neil Carpathios, "No More Same Old Silly Love Songs," from *Beyond the Bones*, FutureCycle Press, 2013. Reprinted with permission of the author.

Neil Carpathios, "Weighing," from *Beyond the Bones*, Future-Cycle Press, 2013. Reprinted with permission of the author.

Billy Collins, "Introduction to Poetry," from *The Apple That Astonished Paris*, The University of Arkansas Press, 1988. Reprinted with permission of The University of Arkansas Press.

Barbara Crooker, "Mowing at Dusk," from *Writing Home*, Gehry Press, 1983. Reprinted with permission of the author.

Jill Eulalie Dawson, "Erithracus Rubecula," from *Scintilla 14* (2010): 62. Reprinted with permission of the author.

Maureen E. Doallas, "Portrait by Matisse," from *Neruda's Memoirs: Poems,* T. S. Poetry Press, 2011. Reprinted with permission of T. S. Poetry Press.

Carmen Gimenèz Smith, "The Daughter," from *Milk & Filth*, The University of Arizona Press, 2013. Reprinted with permission of the author.

Bob Hicok, "My Life with a Gardener," from *Insomnia Diary*, University of Pittsburgh Press, 2004. Reprinted with permission of University of Pittsburgh Press.

Maria Hummel, "One Life," from *House and Fire, American Poetry Review*, 2013. Reprinted with permission of the author.

Erin Keane, "The Gravity Soundtrack," from *The Gravity Soundtrack*, WordFarm, 2007. Reprinted with permission of WordFarm and the author.

Marci Rae Johnson & Yvonne Robery, "The Pants of Existence," from *Every Day Poems* (November, 2012). Reprinted with permission of the authors.

Richard Maxson, "SRV in the Parking Lot at the Quick Stop," from *Every Day Poems* (July, 2013). Reprinted with permission of the author.

Pamela Miller, "The Body Reinvented," from *Miss Unthinkable*, Mayapple Press, 2013. Reprinted with permission of the author.

Benjamin Myers, "A Love Poem," from *Elegy for Trains*, Village Books Press, 2010. Reprinted with permission of the author.

Benjamin Myers, "Blessing," from *Elegy for Trains*, Village Books Press, 2010. Reprinted with permission of the author.

Benjamin Myers, "Loss," from *Lapse Americana*, New York Quarterly Books, 2013. Reprinted with permission of the author.

Anne M. Doe Overstreet, "Gathered," from *Delicate Machinery Suspended*, T. S. Poetry Press, 2011. Reprinted with permission of T. S. Poetry Press.

Anne M. Doe Overstreet, "Men Who Love the Domed Heads of Old Dogs," from *Delicate Machinery Suspended*, T. S. Poetry

Press, 2011. Reprinted with permission of T. S. Poetry Press.

Patrick Phillips, "Matinee," from *Boy*, University of Georgia Press, 2008. Reprinted with permission of the author.

Melissa Stein, "Want Me," from *Rough Honey, American Poetry Review*, Copper Canyon Press, 2010. Reprinted with permission of the author.

Jeffrey Thomson, "Fabulous Ones," from *Birdwatching in Wartime*, Carnegie Mellon University Press, 2009. Reprinted with permission of the author.

Sholeh Wolpé, "Prelude," *Keeping Time with Blue Hyacinths*, The University of Arkansas Press, 2013. Reprinted with permission of the author.

David Wright, "Phoenix," from *Every Day Poems*, (May, 2013). Reprinted with permission of the author.

Also from T. S. Poetry Press

Rumors of Water: Thoughts on Creativity & Writing, by L.L. Barkat (Twice named a Best Book of 2011)

A few brave writers pull back the curtain to show us their creative process. Annie Dillard did this. So did Hemingway. Now L.L. Barkat has given us a thoroughly modern analysis of writing. Practical, yes, but also a gentle uncovering of the art of being a writer.

— Gordon Atkinson, Editor at Laity Lodge

Spin: Taking Your Creativity to the Nth Degree, by Claire Burge

A talisman on your creative journey. It will be your friend for life.

—Mary Carty, author of *50 Monster Ideas;* CEO of Spoiltchild, a BAFTA Nominated Design Agency

The Whipping Club, by Deborah Henry (an Oprah selection)

Multilayered themes of prejudice, corruption and redemption with an authentic voice and swift, seamless dialogue. A powerful saga of love and survival.

—*Kirkus Reviews* (starred review)

Field Guide Series

The Field Guide Series tutors on a practical level—
in matters of reading, writing, or the development
of writing careers.

T. S. Poetry Press titles are available online in e-book and print
editions. Print editions also available through Ingram.

tspoetry.com

CPSIA information can be obtained
at www.ICGtesting.com
Printed in the USA
LVHW051352220123
737703LV00003B/610

9 780989 854221